For violin
Für Violine

Nifty Shifts

Tunes and technical tips to kick-start position changing
Stücke und Übungen für einen gelungenen Einstieg in den Lagenwechsel

Mary Cohen

© 2004 by Faber Music Ltd
First published in 2004 by Faber Music Ltd
Bloomsbury House 74–77 Great Russell Street London WC1B 3DA
Music processed by MusicSet 2000
Cover and illustrations by Todd O'Neill
Design by Susan Clarke
Printed in England by Caligraving Ltd

ISBN10: 0-571-52187-8
EAN13: 978-0-571-52187-6

To buy Faber Music publications or to find out about the full range of titles available
please contact your local music retailer or Faber Music sales enquiries:

Faber Music Ltd, Burnt Mill, Elizabeth Way, Harlow CM20 2HX
Tel: +44 (0) 1279 82 89 82   Fax: +44 (0) 1279 82 89 83
sales@fabermusic.com   fabermusic.com

FABER *ff* MUSIC

Getting started

Zu Beginn

You may be surprised to learn that you probably already know most of the skills necessary for position work! This book will help you to perfect these skills, and to find extra (or 'transferable') uses for them.

Vielleicht überrascht es dich: Das meiste, was du für den Lagenwechsel brauchst, kennst du wahrscheinlich schon. Dieses Heft wird dir dabei helfen, auf schon vorhandenen Grundlagen aufzubauen und darüber hinaus neue Wege zu finden.

Transferable skills

Technische Voraussetzungen

- Glissandi up and down the fingerboard
  Glissandi auf dem Griffbrett nach oben und unten

- Finding the harmonics halfway along each string
  Obertöne in der Mitte der leeren Saite finden

- Playing in tune in lots of different keys in 1st position
  Sauberes Spiel in verschiedenen Tonarten in der 1. Lage

- Using the 4th finger to replace an open string
  Durch Greifen mit dem 4. Finger die leere Saite ersetzen

- Being able to play in tune on a violin that is several sizes too small for you!
  Sauberes Spiel auf einer Geige, die deutlich zu klein für dich ist!

The science bit

Zum physikalisch-technischen Hintergrund

When you play in 1st position, you are working with the length of string stretching from the bridge to the nut – so all the gaps between your fingertips relate to this 'open' string length. When you play 'stopped' notes (i.e. not harmonics) in positions further up the fingerboard, the length of the string is shortened – so the gaps between the fingertips need to be adjusted. (You would do this automatically if you were trying to play in tune on a tiny violin!)

Beim Spiel in der 1. Lage setzt du die zwischen Steg und Griffbrettsattel gespannte Saite ein. Die Abstände der Finger stehen in Relation zur Länge dieser leeren Saite. Beim Spiel gegriffener Töne in höheren Lagen (also nicht von Flageolett-Tönen) wird die Länge der Saite verkürzt, so dass die Abstände zwischen den Fingern entsprechend angepasst werden müssen. (Beim Spiel auf einer viel zu kleinen Geige würdest du das automatisch tun!)

Dynamic markings have been deliberately left out, so you can concentrate fully on shifting. Bowing has been kept to a minimum too, but once you become confident, try adding in your own dynamics and bowing.

Dynamische Angaben sind absichtlich weggelassen, sodass man sich völlig auf die Lagenwechsel konzentrieren kann. Die Bogenführungen sind auch minimal eingefügt. Wenn sicher, kann man versuchen seine eigenen dynamischen Angaben und Bogenführungen hinzuzufuegen.

Look out for these symbols as you work through this book:

Achte beim Arbeiten mit dem Heft auf die folgenden Zeichen:

 Work out the fingering
Fingersatz ausarbeiten

 Get a finger in position ready to play
Den Finger zum Greifen vorbereiten

 Mark in the semitones
Die Halbtöne markieren

 Play by ear
Nach dem Gehör spielen

 Listen to your playing
Dem eigenen Spiel lauschen

 Shift
Lagenwechsel

 Bright idea
Gute Idee!

 Keep your fingernails short, and your hands and the violin neck as clean as possible.
Deine Fingernägel hältst du am besten kurz; deine Hände und der Hals der Violine sollten so sauber wie möglich sein!

Frère Jacques

- Playing a well-known tune in different keys
  Eine bekannte Melodie in verschiedenen Tonarten spielen

- Developing use of the 4th finger in 1st position
  Den Einsatz des 4. Fingers in der 1. Lage trainieren

D major, 1st position D-Dur, 1. Lage

Trad.

E major, 1st position E-Dur, 1. Lage

Use 4th finger *4. Finger verwenden*

B♭ major, 1st position B-Dur, 1. Lage

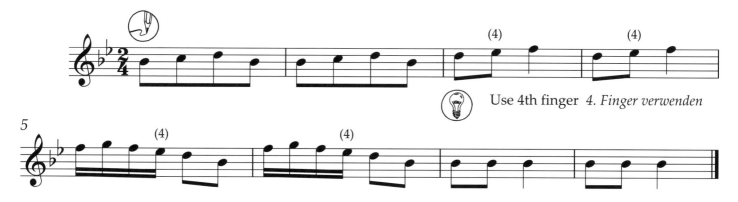

Use 4th finger *4. Finger verwenden*

- Finishing a well-known tune in 1st position by ear, then in 3rd position
  Eine bekannte Melodie in der ersten Lage nach dem Gehör zu Ende spielen, dann in der 3. Lage

- Writing in 3rd position fingering
  Schreib den Fingersatz für die 3. Lage dazu!

A♭ major, 1st position   As-Dur, 1. Lage

Now get ready to play the incredible shrinking violin!
Und jetzt kannst du gleich auf einer immer kleiner werdenden Geige spielen!

1 Play D in 1st position
Den Ton D in der 1. Lage spielen

2 Memorise the sound
Stell dir den Ton vor

3 Find and play D in 3rd position
Such und spiel den Ton D in der 3. Lage

4 Check it still sounds the same
Kontrolliere, ob es noch gleich klingt

5 Remember that the violin has 'shrunk' so your fingers should be closer together
Denk dran, dass die Violine „geschrumpft" ist, deine Finger sollten also dichter beisammen liegen

 You might like to try some 'Glisserobics' here. See page 15.
Vielleicht möchtest du hier einige „Glisserobics" ausprobieren (vgl. S.15)

D major, 3rd position   D-Dur, 3. Lage

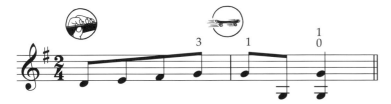

G major, 3rd position   G-Dur, 3. Lage

Test 1st finger against open G
Vergleiche den 1. Finger mit der leeren G-Saite

5

Can Can

- Another well-known tune in 1st position, then in 3rd position
  Noch eine bekannte Melodie, erst in der 1., dann in der 3. Lage

- Preparation exercises to find starting notes in 3rd position
  Vorbereitende Übungen, um Anfangstöne in der 3. Lage zu finden

A major, 1st position A-Dur, 1. Lage

Jacques Offenbach

A major, 1st position A-Dur, 1. Lage

Remember to use your 4th finger where marked – you won't have the choice of open strings in higher positions.

Denk dran, den 4. Finger wo vorgeschrieben zu verwenden – in höheren Lagen gibt es nicht die Alternative der leeren Saiten.

Can you play this version of the Can Can from memory?
Kannst du diese Version des Cancan auswendig spielen?

... in 3rd position too! ... auch in der 3. Lage!

D major, 3rd position   D-Dur, 3. Lage

G major, 3rd position   G-Dur, 3. Lage

C major, 3rd position   C-Dur, 3. Lage

Morning has broken

• Developing confidence in 3rd position
Sicherheit in der 3. Lage entwickeln

G major, 1st position   G-Dur, 1. Lage

Ode to joy

G major, 1st position   G-Dur, 1. Lage

You might like to try some 'Fingerobics' here. See page 14.
Vielleicht möchtest du einige „Fingerobics" probieren. Siehe Seite 14.

Ludwig van Beethoven

- Preparation exercises with the semitone in a new place
  Vorbereitende Übungen mit dem Halbton an einer neuen Stelle
- Extensive use of 4th finger in a well-known tune
  Häufig eingesetzter 4. Finger bei einer bekannten Melodie

G major, 3rd position   G-Dur, 3. Lage

> Use your left elbow to help place your left thumb, so your fingers can reach the fingerboard easily.
> Mit dem linken Ellbogen kannst du dir beim Platzieren des linken Daumens helfen; dann erreichen deine Finger das Griffbrett leicht.

C major, 3rd position   C-Dur, 3. Lage

2nd movement, Symphony No. 9 'From the New World'

- Further development of preparation strategies
  Weitere vorbereitende Übungen in der 1. Lage
- Shifting to and from 3rd position within a piece – during a rest, or via an open string
  Wechsel aus und in die 3. Lage innerhalb eines Stückes – während einer Pause oder auf dem Weg über eine leere Saite

D major, 1st position   D-Dur, 1. Lage

Antonin Dvořák

D major, 3rd and 1st positions   D-Dur, 3. und 1. Lage

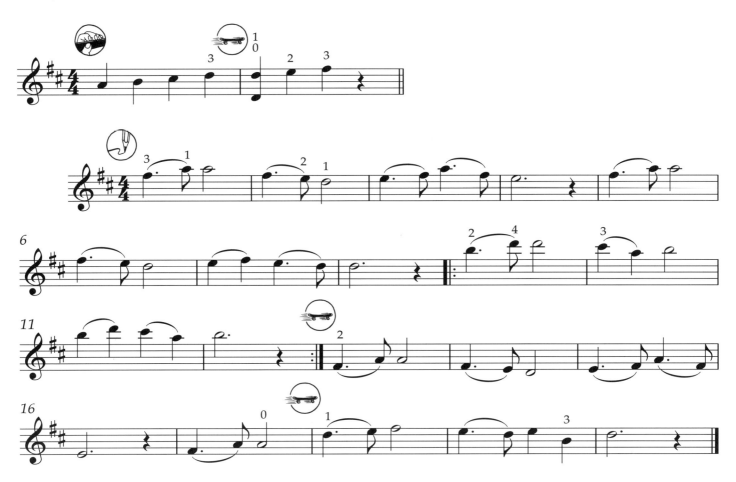

It's often possible to shift during a rest or while playing an open string. (See also page 16 for exercises introducing a 'guide' finger.)

Häufig ist ein Lagenwechsel während einer Pause oder auf der leeren Saite möglich (siehe auch S. 16 für Übungen mit einem „Leit"-Finger.)

'Minuet' from Music for the royal fireworks

• Starting a piece in 1st position, then shifting to and from 3rd position
Ein Stück in der 1. Lage beginnen, dann Lagenwechsel in die 3. und zurück

D major, 1st and 3rd positions   D-Dur, 1. und 3. Lage

George Frideric Handel

* Stay in position
* Handstellung nicht verändern

'La rejouissance' from Music for the royal fireworks

• Once you are confident with the shifting, try adding in some dynamics.
Wenn sicher, kann man versuchen seine eigenen dynamischen Angaben hinzuzufuegen.

D major, 1st and 3rd positions   D-Dur, 1. und 3. Lage

 Practise the tricky 3rd position sections in 1st position first
Üb die schwierigen Abschnitte in der 3. Lage zunächst in der 1. Lage!

George Frideric Handel

Shift via open string
Lagenwechsel über die leere Saite

Fingerobics

• A sequence to develop finger dexterity and intonation
  skills, working up from B♭ major to G major
  Eine Übung zur Verbesserung von Geschicklichkeit und
  Intonationssicherheit, von B-Dur nach G-Dur

Glisserobics

• Exercises to develop relaxation during the mechanics of shifting
Übungen zur besseren Entspannung während des eigentlichen Lagenwechsels

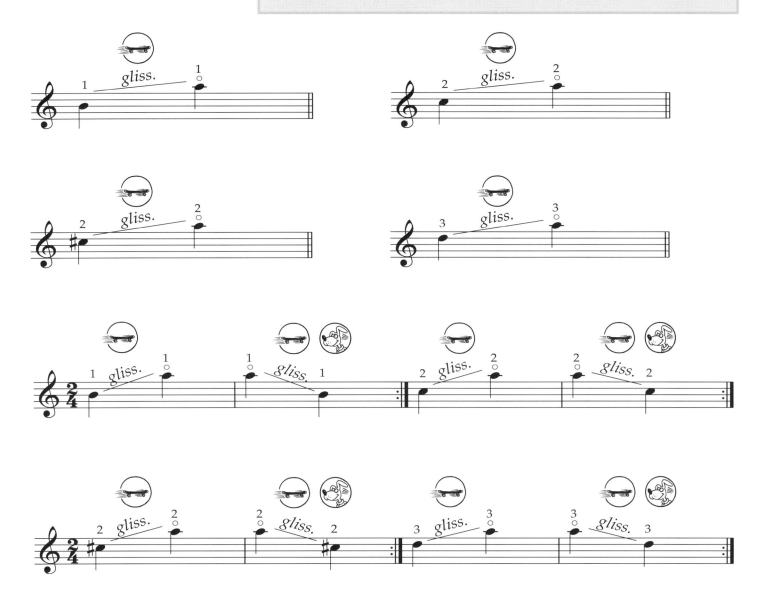

 Make up more 'glisserobics' on the other strings.
Erfinde weitere „Glisserobics" auf den anderen Saiten.

 Harmonic pressure
Leichter Fingeraufsatz für Flageolett-Töne

1 Imagine both arms are floating in the sea, so the violin and bow feel almost weightless.
Stell dir vor, dass beide Arme im Meer schweben, Geige und Bogen sind fast gewichtslos.

2 As you go from 1st position to the harmonic, notice that your left hand comes towards you from the left, slightly towards your middle – and slightly downhill!
Beim Wechsel aus der 1. Lage zum Flageolett spürst du, dass die linke Hand sich dir von links her nähert, ein wenig zu dir hin und ein bisschen nach unten!

3 Make the return journey so your hand goes back to exactly the spot it started from – it should start from your middle and go out slightly to the left, uphill!
Beim Rückweg soll deine Hand den Weg genau zurückverfolgen, um wieder da zu landen, wo sie herkam. Die Bewegung sollte von deiner Mitte aus starten und leicht nach links aufwärts führen!

4 If you remember to do this return journey accurately, it prevents the violin drooping as your hand travels up and down the fingerboard.
Wenn du diesen Rückweg sorgfältig ausführst, vermeidest du das Absinken der Geige, während die Hand auf dem Griffbrett auf und abwandert.

Shifty bits and pieces
Allerlei Lagenwechsel

• Introducing the use of a guide finger during the shift
Einführen eines „Leit-Fingers" während des Lagenwechsels

D major scale D-Dur Tonleiter
1st position 1. Lage

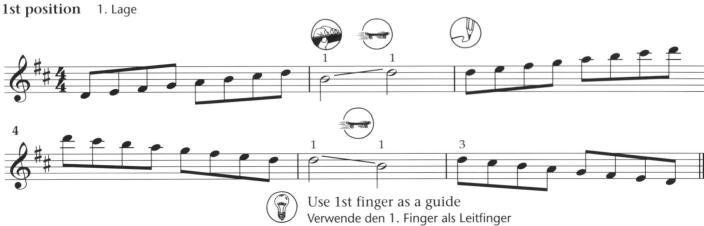

Use 1st finger as a guide
Verwende den 1. Finger als Leitfinger

D major arpeggio D-Dur-Arpeggio
1st and 3rd positions 1. und 3. Lage

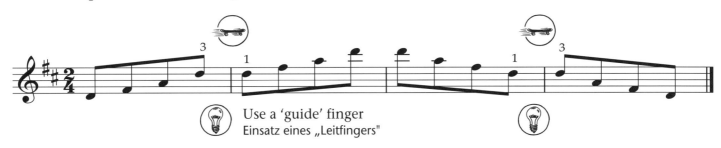

Use a 'guide' finger
Einsatz eines „Leitfingers"

D minor scale d-Moll-Tonleiter
1st and 3rd positions 1. und 3. Lage

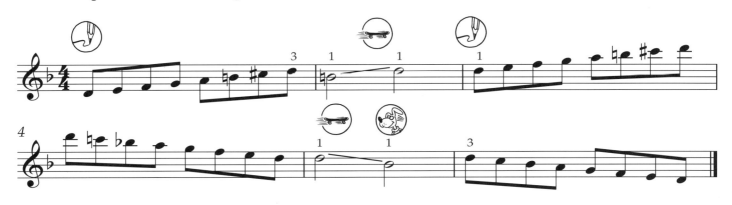

D minor arpeggio d-Moll-Arpeggio

Use a 'guide' finger
Einsatz eines „Leitfingers"